WORKBOOK FOR

LIKE A RIVER

(A Guide to Granger Smith's Book)

Your Powerful Guide on Finding the Faith and Strength to Move Forward after Loss and Heartache

ABOUT GRANGER SMITH

Granger Smith, a country singer and songwriter from Dallas, started his professional music career as a freshman at Texas A&M with the release of his debut album, 1998's Waiting on Forever. Five further studio albums (all written, recorded, and produced by Smith in his home studio), self-released over the next 15 years, led to widespread distribution of 2013's Dirt Road Driveway. In 2015, with the release of the 4x4 EP, he finally found success with three Top 20 country singles.

After that successful decade, he continued to release popular albums into the next one, including 2017's When the Good Guys Win and 2020's Country Things. In 2022, Smith released Moonrise, his eleventh studio album.

Smith, who had been performing on the Texas circuit since the age of 14, launched his professional recording career when he was 19 years old.

While still a freshman at Texas A&M, he recorded his first album, Waiting on Forever, and two years later he got a writing and publishing deal with EMI Music Publishing. He dropped out of school in the middle of his junior year to move to Music City, where he spent his time performing in bars and clubs while learning the ropes of songwriting and recording.

In 2005, Smith graduated from Texas A&M and self-published his second album, Memory RD. He also released

Pockets of Pesos that year. A year later, in 2006, came Livin' Like a Lonestar, and a year after that, in 2007, came We Bleed Maroon.

Smith had returned to his native state of Texas by this point and was performing regularly to the point where he was a great star on the Texas circuit.

The first CD, 2009's Don't Listen to the Radio, was followed by two more in 2012: Live at the Chicken: 11-20-

11 and Poets & Prisoners. Songs like "Country Boy Love" and "The Country Boy Song," written by Smith's comic alter ego Earl Dibbles, Jr., may be found on his 2013 album Dirt Road Driveway.

As of 2015, "Backroad Song" was a Top Ten country hit and peaked at number one on Billboard's Country Airplay charts, while the four-song EP 4x4 reached number six on the Country Albums chart and number fifty-one on the Top 200 Albums listing. After being awarded Taste of Country's 2016 Hottest Artist to Watch in January, Smith's major label debut album, Remington, was released in March.

When the Good Guys Win, Smith's eighth studio album, was released the following year, and it featured the hit single "Happens Like That." Smith released a film and score for They Were There, A Hero's Documentary in 2018.

Granger Smith issued a set of EPs in 2020 titled Country Things, Vol. 1 and Country Things, Vol. 2, and then compiled them into a single LP titled Country Things.

Smith and High Valley's collaboration on the track "Country Music, Girls and Trucks," released in support of their 2022 album Moonrise, was a huge success in Canada.

**THIS ONE WEEK OUTLINE WAS
DEVELOPED TO HELP YOU.**

➢ The foremost thing
is to find a
person you can rely on to
help you achieve your
goals if you want to be
successful.

➢ Be careful not
to make any mistakes
when filling out the vital
forms displayed below.

➢ Consider each day's tip, task and prescription carefully.

THINK ABOUT THEM MEDITATIVELY.

➢ Everything you learned in the note should be written and meditated upon.

Also, jot down your thoughts and feelings, as well as the obstacles you've come to terms with.

READ AND LISTEN TO EVERYTHING THAT IS BEING SAID AND RECOMMENDED.

Without a doubt, adhere to them.

IT WAS MADE TO BE POSSIBLE.

**Never doubt the fact that you
can do it, and never give up hope.**

**YOU'RE ALL SET TO STEP
ON TO THE NEXT LEVEL!**

Ensure that you fill out the Form below in its entirety.

DATE IT ALL BEGINS

_____

_____

DATE OF FINAL CONCLUSION (Usually 7 D ays from the starting Date)

Fill in the blanks with your name and email address:

FILL OUT YOUR AGE

It's not as difficult as you might

**think, but don't take it for
granted and keep going.**

**Recommendations and
Tasks for the Day Don't End
That Day; Carry On and
Make Habits of Them.**

DAY 1

INSIGHT

A very necessary move to take in your
battle against trauma is your ability to
accept support. Although you might
be feeling down in those times, don't

underrate the power of a helping hand.

WHAT YOU SHOULD IMBIBE TODAY

Embrace the love, care and support you receive from genuine people around you. Don't treat them badly.

DON'T FORGET...

You can't possibly fight this battle
just by yourself, you need help.

MEDITATE

_____

_____

_____

_____

_____

_____

_____

_____

_____

_____

_____

_____

_____

_____

No man is an Island.

DAY 2

INSIGHT

After adjusting your psych to be able
to accept help from truly concerned

people, it is necessary for you to identify the type of help you need. You can do this by identifying the type of problem you're facing.

WHAT YOU SHOULD IMBIBE TODAY...

Discover what others can do that'd assist you best. Make them know for maximum impact.

DON'T FORGET...

Don't let those caring for you labor in
vain, tell them the exact things your
needs are.

MEDITATE

_____
_____
_____
_____
_____

_____

_____

_____

_____

_____

_____

_____

Finding out your problems makes help more effective.

<u>DAY 3</u>

<u>INSIGHT</u>

Build connection and relationship with positive, mature and friendly people. Spend your time around them and forget your sorrows.

<u>WHAT YOU SHOULD IMBIBE TODAY</u>

Maintaining a good social network plays an important role when it comes to battling trauma. Find yours now.

DON'T FORGET...

Always hang around the right people, don't compromise this.

MEDITATE...

_____

_____

_____

_____

_____

_____

_____

_____

_____

_____

_____

_____

**Make friends that are
capable of assisting you
during your dark days.**

DAY 4

INSIGHT

Even if the world treats you badly,
you should never treat yourself same
way. This period practice self-care
like never before.

WHAT YOU SHOULD IMBIBE TODAY

Frequently take yourself out for treats,
do those healthy things that make you
happy. Have a reason to be happy.

<u>DON'T FORGET...</u>

The way you treat yourself has the greatest lasting effect on the long run.

MEDITATE

_____

_____

_____

_____

_____

_____

_____

_____

_____

_____

_____

_____

_____

Be happy, It is in your control to be.

DAY 5

INSIGHT

Don't go about seeking solace in hard drugs, alcohol or any other recreational substance. Realize now that it'd only compound your situation, it'd make things worse.

<u>WHAT YOU SHOULD IMBIBE TODAY...</u>

Keep hard drugs, alcohol and cigarette far from sight or scent. Keep friends who patronize these things far.

<u>DON'T FORGET</u>

These substances would not help you.
They're like time bombs, they'd
surely boomerang when the time is
right.

MEDITATE

_____

_____

_____

_____

_____

_____

_____

_____

_____

_____

_____

_____

_____

_____

_____
_____
_____
_____
_____
_____
_____
_____
_____
_____
_____
_____

Say no to hard drugs!

<u>DAY 6</u>

INSIGHT

Taking breaks from time to time is very necessary when it comes to healing from trauma. The process could be exhausting, pause by and rest.

WHAT YOU SHOULD IMBIBE TODAY

As you strive towards recovery, never forget to pause by and rest each time it looks like the weight on you is so much.

<u>DON'T FORGET</u>

Rest gives you strength to continue, it
has healing effect that heals.

MEDITATE

_____

_____

_____

_____

_____

_____

_____

_____

_____

_____

_____

Catch your breath!!!

DAY 7

INSIGHT

The period of recovery from trauma remains among the best time in a person's life to practice self-improvement. Use this time to level up. Master a skill, master it furiously and become successful from it.

WHAT YOU SHOULD IMBIBE TODAY

Find a skill based on your talent, devote your energy on it, master it and make money from it.

<u>DON'T FORGET</u>

Channeling your time and effort
learning a new skill channels away
the energy of depression and changes
it for your own good.

MEDITATE

_____

_____

_____

_____

_____

_____

_____

_____

_____

_____

_____

_____

Trauma could turn out to be your biggest motivation!!!

YOU'VE FINISHED WITHTHIS ONE WEEK GUIDE. KEEP UP WITH IT.

POSITIVE RESULT COMES WITH IT.

Show Love to people by giving them copies of this.

_____

_____

_____

_____

_____

_____

_____

_____

_____

_____

_____

_____

_____

_____

_____

BYE!

Each time you're deviating, return to this!

Made in the USA
Columbia, SC
13 August 2024

40389700R00026